"It's O.K. *to Say* No! is a wonderful resource for group leaders, teachers and parents to utilize in instructing children about protecting themselves from those who might victimize them. The book is clever, appealing and entertaining and reinforces learning through discussions, stories and pictures. An excellent book!"

—Sister Georgianna Cahill, SSS, LCSW
Administrative Director
Catholic Youth & Community Service

"It's O.K. *to Say* No! is a practical form of child sexual abuse prevention. It is a must for parents as well as teachers. Direct and to the point, it offers solid 'how to' suggestions in real-life situations."

—Barbara Griffith, Ph.D.
Clinical Psychologist
Editor for Region Nine Children,
Youth and Families Resource Center,
Los Angeles, CA

"It's O. K. *To Say* No!... treads the middle ground between cynicism and optimism in dealing with a painful topic. While it intends to make children wary, it does not intend for parents to shift the full burden of responsibility for the personal, physical safety of children to the children themselves."

—*School Library Journal*

"An extremely valuable prevention tool for children and parents alike. We can only provide positive words for the content of this publication."

—Robin E. Swank
    Volunteers Against Abuse Center

"The book deals sensitively with its subject, and although it may be unpleasant initially, it will ease everyone's anxiety in the end. Now parents have a tool that they can use in teaching their kids. Especially important is the fact that the book helps get parents and children actively involved."

—Dr. Regina Pally
    Chairman of the Women's Committee
    of the Southern California
    Psychiatric Society
    Faculty member, UCLA

IT'S O.K. TO SAY NO!

A PARENT/CHILD MANUAL FOR THE PROTECTION OF CHILDREN

ROBIN LENETT with BOB CRANE

Illustrated by FRANK C. SMITH

AN RGA PRODUCTION

With very special thanks for their help in the preparation of this book to Lt. Richard D. Willey and Sergeant Beth Dickinson of the Los Angeles County Shriff's Department, Child Abuse Detail.

Our special thanks also to Dana Barthelme, without whom this book could not have been written.

The stories in chapter five are works of fiction. All the characters and events portrayed in this chapter and in other examples in this book are fictional. Any resemblance to real people in this book are fictional. Any resemblance to real people or incidents is purely coincidental.

IT'S O.K. TO SAY NO!

First printing: July 1985
Sixth Printing: June 1994

Cover art by Matt Stawicki

ISBN: 1-55902-986-2

Printed in the United States of America

0 9 8 7 6

Chapter One

At the rate of every two minutes in the United States, a child is sexually abused. It means that in the time it will take you to read this book, sixty more children will have been sexually abused.

Those chilling facts tell only part of the story. For every case reported to authorities, the sexual abuse of ten to twenty more children may go undisclosed. Experts estimate that one out of three girls and one out of seven boys will have been sexually abused by the time they reach the age of eighteen.

Sexual assault on children has been aptly called "the hidden crime" —hidden because many children, out of fear or shame, are reluctant to tell of their experiences; hidden because many parents, for their own reasons, fail to report instances of sexual abuse to the proper authorities; hidden because the damage often is not evident, although the psychological scars may remain for a lifetime.

In the past several years, instances of child sexual abuse have become front-page news. The seemingly sudden emergence of this crime has caused some people to believe that this is a new and tragic twist in our sexually permissive times.

The crime of child sexual assault, however, is probably as old as the human race. It was commonplace in every ancient civilization, including those that are looked upon as enlightened for their times. Clay tablets thousands of years old record instances of the sexual abuse of children.

Even in Victorian times—erroneously considered a period of sexual decorum—the sexual exploitation of children was a suppressed scandal of enormous proportions. Throughout Europe the kidnapping of children for sexual purposes was an epidemic, allowed to occur because society refused to accept the reality of such unthinkable practices.

Experts say that our heightened awareness of the extent and consequences of child sexual abuse stems from our willingness to confront troubling social issues. In the past decade, our society has come to grips with many sexually related issues that were once only whispered about in private conversation. You have only to scan a week's television schedule to recognize how open we've become about sexual matters.

The sexual abuse of children seems to be the last frontier in the public discussion of sexual matters. We quite naturally turn from it with a sense of revulsion. The subject is painful. Ours is a society that cherishes the concept of the innocence of childhood, a society that idealizes childhood as a time of sugarplums and candy.

Children are taught about the dangers of crossing the street, the risks of poisonous substances, the hazards of playing with matches. No one assumes that these lessons undermine the innocence of childhood.

Children can similarly be taught some basic lessons that will help them deal with an attempted sexual abuse. The sexual abuse of children cannot be totally prevented—any more than we can fully shield our children from automobiles, poisons, and fire—but we can at least arm them with a rudimentary awareness of how to deal with an instance of potential assault.

Such awareness offers no guarantees, but it at least reduces the risks.

Chapter Two

Who are the people
who sexually molest children?

We can't draw a profile of the typical offender. They come from all walks of life. Many are highly respected members of the community. Some are in positions of authority over children—teachers, doctors, police officers, clergymen, coaches.

Statistics on age are meaningless. Identified child molesters range from early teens to the nineties.

We do have some insights, however. Approximately nineteen out of twenty identified sexual abusers of children are male. About half of them are married, with children of their own. The national average age of known child molesters is twenty-nine.

The common image of the typical child molester as a stranger is largely a myth. The majority of child molesters know their victims. They are relatives, family friends, neighbors, or someone else the victim routinely comes in contact with.

Most identified child molesters were themselves sexually abused as children. The desire to sexually abuse children is a sexual preference, not unlike homosexuality or heterosexuality. The offender generally prefers sexual contact with children to any other form of sexual expression, even though he may have sexual relationships within his own peer group.

For that reason, it is very rare that a child molester commits only one such crime. A recent study of convicted child molesters shows that the average offender sexually abuses more than seventy children before being apprehended.

Psychiatric counseling of convicted child molesters has produced valuable information about their modes of conduct and how they select their victims.

Because the abuse of children is a sexual preference formed relatively early in life, some offenders consciously or unconsciously choose career paths that will bring them regularly in contact with children. Others may volunteer to supervise children's sports or club activities.

The child molester typically possesses a devious cunning. Those in positions of child supervision often work diligently to build an exemplary record of competence in their activities. Such a record serves two purposes for them. First, it heightens their esteem in the eyes of parents, who express that esteem to their children, thus making it easier for the offender to abuse the children in his or her charge. Second, an exemplary record can serve as a defense if an abused child speaks out. Members of the community will often point to the offender's record and refuse to believe the child.

A typical example is a baseball coach who sexually abused the most vulnerable of his players but treated the others with exceptional care. When his abusive behavior was reported, the other boys stood up for him and the parents refused to believe the charges, even after it was disclosed that the coach had been previously convicted of child sexual abuse.

Offenders choose their victims with care. If they are working with a group of children, they usually will select as a target the child who is particularly shy and withdrawn, the one who seems the most naive, or the one who has no close friends in the group.

The molester, under any circumstances, may seek out the child who can be isolated, the one who is habitually late being picked up from school or meetings, who tends to linger alone after school or other activities.

The ability to isolate a child is critically important in the molester's schemes. If two or more children are privy to an incident, the chances of disclosure rise dramatically. The molester knows that one child's story may not be believed, but two children telling the identical story will be.

The experts say that child molesters who are not members of the immediate family feel no guilt about their activities. Because the abuse of children is a sexual preference—an inner drive—offenders usually do not feel that they are doing anything wrong. That may be the most chilling element of this tragic crime.

If forced to defend their activities, some child molesters will say

that what they are doing is "good for children." Others will blame the victim by suggesting that the child shared responsibility for the crime. That argument probably has been used by child molesters since time immemorial as an excuse for their actions—and it is brazen nonsense. "She lured me on" or "He didn't try to stop me" are lines heard repeatedly in the prosecution of child molesters.

The experts stress that there is *never* an instance in which a child shares responsibility in any way for sexual abuse. Children are simply the tragic victims of a deviant sexual drive.

Furthermore, a child should always be believed when he or she relates a story of an abuse situation. We all know that children are capable of making up stories and fantasizing, but we also realize that a youngster can only report the specifics of an abuse if it actually occurred.

CHAPTER THREE

What makes it difficult for children to deal with instances of sexual abuse?

Essentially, it's because children inherently trust their elders, and because they are taught to respect authority figures.

To a child, almost anyone more than a few years older than he or she is an authority figure.

It is one thing for a child to talk back to Mom or Dad—for the child knows the consequences of the action. It is another thing altogether to talk back to any other authority figure. A child would anticipate a truly severe penalty if Mom or Dad heard about it.

That necessary respect for authority figures also leaves a child vulnerable to someone who wants to take advantage of the situation.

A child's highly developed sense of trust and respect for authority erodes with experience. In effect, a child must learn to be distrustful of adults, and must learn that authority does not automatically carry the mantle of infallibility.

To help our children protect themselves, we must speed up the learning process a little bit. We must teach our children that they do sometimes have the right to question authority, and that not all adults are to be trusted without hesitation.

On his or her own, a child simply does not have the resources to cope with a beguiling molester. Let's look at a real-life example.

As a child leaves school, a stranger in a parked car calls him over. The stranger says, "Your mother couldn't get here to pick you up, so she asked me to do it. Get in."

Unless the child has been given specific instructions to the contrary, he will probably get into the car without a second thought. First, here is an adult—an authority figure—telling him what to do. Worse, the

instructions uttered by the man are implicitly from the child's mother, giving him additional authority.

The child has little reason to distrust the man, so why would the boy give the circumstances a second thought, other than to wonder what delayed his mother?

This is a good example of the methodology of the child molester. He's well aware of his status as an authority figure in a child's eyes. He also knows that a child's innate sense of trust encourages the acceptance of almost all but the most implausible stories used for enticement.

The molester has an additional powerful advantage over his victim—fear. In a world controlled by adults, and at a substantial physical disadvantage, a child is relatively powerless in his or her relationships with adults.

If a stranger molests a child, he needn't explicitly threaten the child physically. Given his or her powerlessness, a child will read a threat of physical harm—even death—into a molester-victim situation.

If the molester is a relative or a friend or a neighbor, the child may not feel in actual physical danger, but that will not lessen his or her overall sense of fear. Molesters who are known to the child will play upon the child's fear that telling about an incident may have far-reaching consequences.

The molester may suggest to the child that he (the molester) will deny the incident; that no one will believe the child; and, as a result, that he or she will lose parental love, or will be held up to the scorn of friends.

Molesters may play upon more specific fears. There have been cases of teachers using the threat of poor grades, or of coaches threatening to deny playing time to team members.

The irony of these situations is that molesters can get away with a series of such threats until one child speaks up, and the previous victims then provide corroborating evidence.

Added to these enumerated fears is the natural reluctance of children to tell their parents about anything "dirty" that they may have been involved in. Child molestations rarely are witnessed by a third person. Thus, the child victim is the only one who can disclose the occurrence of a molestation.

The molester works with three advantages in victimizing children—

the victims' respect for authority, trust in adults, and fear of the consequences of resisting or telling about an incident.

If we are to arm our children with some defensive capabilities, we must deal with each of those elements.

In our society, many adults deserve respect from children. We must teach our children that a few adults may attempt to take advantage of their status.

Children should be taught that being respected carries an obligation to act in a respectable manner. Respect is a two-way street. The child respects the adult, but has the right to demand respect in return. Children should be taught that anyone who attempts to get a child to do something that the child knows is improper forfeits the right to respect.

You must keep in mind that misplaced respect is one of the leading contributors to our inability to reduce the number of child molestations that occur. Society is still too willing to excuse this crime when it is committed by a "respected" member of the community.

Your child must be made to realize that adults are not always trustworthy. That may not be as difficult as it might seem. You can teach your child that "even 'good' people sometimes do bad things." In teaching that lesson to your child, you may be able to draw upon his or her experiences to make your case. You can project your child's experiences with playmates to an adult level to get your points across.

Dealing with the element of fear has some limitations. There is no way to make a child less fearful of physical harm in potentially dangerous encounters with adults.

The other kinds of fear used by molesters can be dealt with successfully. Essentially, they arise from a child's assumption that disclosure of an incident of abuse will mean scorn for him or her, or a loss of parental love.

Clearly, such fears are unfounded. If that is the case, why do so many children seem to believe that disclosure will have devastating consequences?

They believe it because of ignorance. They believe it because, unless they are told otherwise, they have no reason to disbelieve it.

Child molesters thrive in an atmosphere of ignorance, secrecy, and anonymity. If we are to protect our children from these criminals, we must educate where there is ignorance, reveal where there is secrecy, and identify where there is anonymity.

17

Chapter Four

What can we do
to protect our children?

There are people who feel that children should be protected from the realities of life as long as possible. Their position would be well taken—if this were an ideal world.

The realization that there are adults in the world who would harm children could be somewhat painful to discuss with your children. However, this could well be the most important discussion you will ever have with them. You owe it to your children to provide them with the basic tools they need to help them in potentially dangerous situations.

Children have lived in anguish over repeated instances of molestation simply because they feared discussing the matter with their parents. The establishment of a climate of frankness between you and your children, an environment in which they feel free to discuss matters of concern to them, is a vital first step in the process of dealing with the potential of child sexual abuse.

A child may feel shame and guilt over an incident, and fear that disclosure may bring parental wrath upon him or her. Or the child may fear that the parent may make the incident public, thus bringing scorn upon the child.

Some children have even been motivated by a desire to spare their parents the pain of knowing that they have been molested. Other children may fear an irrational parental reaction. Counselors have heard variations on the following line: "I was afraid to tell my parents because I knew my father would go after the guy and try to kill him."

Ideally you should create an environment in your home in which a child feels free to openly discuss with you any encounters he or she may have with adults. How do you help foster such an environment?

Probably the most important element is your own attitude. If you dismiss as inconsequential all of the minor concerns expressed to you by your child, he or she is likely to be less than forthright about issues of major concern.

Keep in mind that a child's comments about even inconsequential matters in their relations with others, whether adults or child friends, may be an early signal of something troubling in a relationship.

A child's lack of experience may make it difficult for him or her to verbalize concerns about the behavior of someone known or encountered by chance. For example, a child may ask, "How come Mr. Shields is always home during the daytime?"

The question may be a perfectly innocent one. You answer, "That's because Mr. Shields works at home." You could leave it at that, or you could take it one step further and say, "Why do you ask?"

The child may reply, "Oh, I don't know. I just see him around a lot."

You could take it another step and ask, "Where do you see him around? Isn't he usually inside?" The conversation may lead nowhere. On the other hand, Mr. Shields could be a child molester, and your child may be sending you an indirect message by wondering aloud why he sees Mr. Shields in different areas of the neighborhood.

We're not suggesting that you become paranoid about the mutterings of children, but if a child asks unusual questions about friends, relatives, neighbors, or the adults who supervise him or her, it may be worthwhile to follow up on those questions.

You help foster an environment of openness by encouraging your child to talk about his or her daily experiences, about friends, and about adults. For example, you might ask, "How is your Little League practice coming along? How do you like your new coach?" If you show a genuine interest in your child's activities, he or she is likely to be frank with you.

Some of the following specific suggestions may seem insignificant. Others may seem extreme. However, all of these suggestions have come from parents who, sadly enough, wish they had discussed them earlier with their children.

This book was written because too many children have been cheated out of their childhoods by adults. We all wish it were not necessary to teach a child that good people can do bad things, but if we want to decrease the number of victims, it is an absolute necessity.

We also intend, through this book, to help prevent another form of

child abuse—that of developing an unnecessary fear of adults and strangers in your child. It is certainly not the intention of this book to keep children from meeting new people or to retard their sense of adventure and curiosity. If your child learns the lessons in this book, under your sensitive guidance, there should be no reason for a change in a healthy, happy attitude toward life.

Is it necessary to convey all of these suggestions to your child? Not necessarily. Choose the ones you feel are most important in your circumstances. You cannot expect your child to learn all of these guidelines.

In teaching your child, stress the suggestions you consider significant. It might be wise to at least discuss the others so that your child develops a sense of awareness.

Some families have found it practical to make "house rules" out of the guidelines that are most important to them. That lifts a burden of responsibility and a decision-making dilemma from the child. For example, if it is a house rule that the child never goes into a neighbor's home without your express approval, the child has no decision to make if the neighbor is insistent, and no responsibility for declining such an invitation.

Probably the most important lesson you can teach your child is that *no one* has the right to touch his or her body. Teach your child that if anyone tries to do so, he or she has the right to say "NO," and should always tell you about it.

Your child should be taught never to go near a car with someone sitting in it. If a stranger in a car calls to him or her, the person should be ignored. If the stranger is asking for directions, he should still be ignored. Tell your child that adults don't turn to children for directions or for help; they turn to other adults.

Your child should be taught that if a stranger approaches for help (finding a lost dog is a common enticement), the child should say "NO," leave the scene, and tell someone about it.

Teach your child to inform you if anyone takes his or her picture, or makes a request to do so. This is another common enticement of the child molester. The police frequently find many candid photos among the effects of convicted child molesters. People don't walk up to strangers, or even acquaintances, and ask to take their pictures for no apparent reason.

You should teach your child to inform you *any time* an adult asks him or her to keep a secret. An adult has no reason to ask a child's confidence (unless there is a very obvious reason for doing so, such as a surprise birthday party for a member of the family).

Teach your child to inform you of any gifts or money offered to him or her by *anyone*.

Your child should be taught never to go into anyone else's home unless you approve it in advance. Children may casually invite friends into their homes, and no one has any second thoughts about it. However, such casual habits can lead to trouble. Get your child into the habit of not going into *anyone's* home without your explicit approval, and you will avoid a potential danger.

Even if the home is that of a trusted friend or neighbor, your child should be taught not to enter, even on the friend's or neighbor's invitation. The child should be told to say "NO," that it is your house rule that he or she cannot enter anyone else's home without your approval. The friend or neighbor will understand.

The same house rule should apply to any automobile. Your child should be taught never to enter any automobile without your express approval. And you should stress to your child that he or she must hear that approval directly from you.

If the people in your neighborhood have a car pool for taking children to and from school, your child should be taught to get into a car driven *only* by one of the people in the car pool. Your child should be taught that specific car-pool drivers are the only people permitted to take the child to and from school. Tell the child that under no circumstances will anyone else be driving, no matter what that person says.

While you're at it, these rules should be stressed to the members of the car pool. Tell them that if a substitute for one of the pool members is sent, your child has been taught not to get into the car, no matter what the driver says.

As soon as he or she is old enough to dial a telephone, teach your child your home phone number, and another number where someone can be reached in case of an emergency. Then teach your child that he or she has the right to use a telephone, without asking anyone's permission, if ever in a situation that is frightening or uncomfortable. You should also explain that the "911" police emergency number is there to help the child in case of a crisis.

24

Your child should be taught never to answer the doorbell when he or she is home alone. The caller probably isn't looking for the child anyway. If it's important, the caller will come back. If it is an emergency situation, the authorities will find a way to get in.

Your child should be taught never to admit on the telephone that he or she is home alone.

If your child picks up the phone and it's a wrong number, he or she should be taught never to give out the number of the phone. If the caller asks, "What number is this?" the child should be taught to ask, "What number are you calling?" When the caller gives the number he or she is trying to reach, the child should be taught to say, "I'm sorry, you have the wrong number," and hang up.

You should teach your child to inform you about any statement made to them, by any person, about love or sex. The reason for that is that some child molesters work very slowly on their victims to gain the child's confidence. They sometimes talk about love or sex as part of their soft sell.

Your child should also be taught to tell you about any unusual discussions, or any requests that seem strange to him or her. These could be early warning signals.

Teach your child that if he or she is ever approached in a store, the child should drop to the floor and scream, "This is not my dad (or my mom)."

Finally, your child should be taught that he or she has the right to say "NO" to *anyone* who puts the child in a situation that feels uncomfortable. And be sure to point out that a "NO" is sufficient in such situations, and that no explanation is necessary.

The latter point is important. Children sometimes fall victim to their inability to articulate a good reason for not doing what has been suggested by an adult. The child says "NO." The adult replies, "But why not?" The child is unable to offer a better reason than "I don't want to," and then falls victim to the adult's rationale.

Tell your child that a "NO" is enough, and explanations are not needed. The child should then simply leave the scene.

There are certain steps that you, as a parent, can take to help establish a protective environment for your child.

First, know the adults your child spends time with during the day. Find out if supervising adults have been subjected to any screening procedures. If your child is in a day-care center, ask the authorities responsible for the center if the employees' histories have been checked. Do local school authorities conduct a background check on new teachers? Fingerprinting of teachers is now being done on a national basis. Is your local school board participating in that program?

If you employ a tutor to give your child private lessons, check into the person's background as well as his or her qualifications. Call the licensing authorities and check references.

Your personal interest in your child's activities can be immeasurably helpful in establishing a protective environment. Keep in mind that anyone intent on sexually abusing a child fears disclosure. Such a person is unlikely to target a child who has a parent actively interested in the child's progress.

That is especially true if the supervising adult believes that a child's activities are being openly discussed at home. You create that impres-

sion by discussing activities from the child's perspective ("Bobby tells me you've been teaching him how to bunt" or "Amy tells me you've been very complimentary about her drawings").

Another suggestion is to be alert for any strong bond that seems to develop between your child and any adult figure in his or her life. If an adult is showing your child an unusual amount of attention, ask yourself why.

Be sensitive to any changes in your child's behavior or attitudes. Such a change may signal the existence of a deeply disturbing situation that your child fears telling you about.

Pay attention if your child says that he or she doesn't want to be with someone in particular. Ask why, and don't attempt to persuade the child otherwise unless the reason is clearly irrational. Even if the child's reason seems to be no more than petulance, it would be worthwhile to follow up with questions about whatever experiences cause the child to feel that way.

Question any money or gifts your child brings home. Ask where they came from, and why they were given.

Don't force a child to submit to physical contact if he or she doesn't want to. Your child may not want to hug Uncle Bob simply because the man has bad breath. That's O.K. By permitting your child to follow his or her instincts in this respect you create the impression that a physical expression of affection is not something adults can demand simply by virtue of their authority.

If you can help it, don't leave your child alone. That isn't easy today, considering the number of two-job households. Under those circumstances, rather than leaving a child alone, either get him or her involved in group activities while you are gone, or put the child in the care of someone you can trust.

Although it may seem an unfair indictment, avoid male baby-sitters for your child. Remember that about ninety-five percent of child molesters are male. By insisting on female baby-sitters, you reduce, but don't always eliminate, the risks by an enormous factor.

Earlier, we discussed the importance of open communication with your child. There are a few guidelines you can follow that will help sustain open communication.

First, never belittle any fear or concern your child may express to you. Remember that the fear articulated by the child may mask a deeper concern.

When a child discloses an incident or fear that may be disturbing him or her, never respond with statements such as "I told you so" or "I never want to hear . . ." They add an element of risk to open disclosure.

Finally, never compromise any private or confidential matter your child may share with you. That also adds an element of risk to open disclosure.

Silence is a child's most damaging response to an incident of sexual abuse. When such an incident occurs, a child needs support, comforting, and professional counseling.

Silence has another chilling consequence. Without disclosure, the molester is encouraged to continue his crimes. One silent victim will lead to yet another victim.

A child's silence is understandable when you consider the numbing fears that cause it. An adult's silence about a known molester is inexplicable. Our society has a baffling tendency to sympathize with the child molester who causes no apparent physical harm.

Think about it. No one sympathizes with a mugger. No one ever says, "Oh, he's mugged a few old ladies, but other than that he seems to be such a nice man."

And yet too many of us seem to rationalize our silence about a "harmless" child molester in precisely that manner. That attitude suggests that while we are unwilling to accept physical harm to our children, we tolerate people who, through sexual abuse, inflict psychological damage.

In all child abuse cases, of both a physical and sexual nature, the psychological scars last a lifetime. Fortunately, with proper counseling and support, an abused child can learn to put the abuse in perspective and lead a happy, productive life.

Chapter Five

On the following pages, you will find a series of stories you can read with your child that will help him or her develop both an awareness of potential dangers and an understanding that it is sometimes okay to say "NO" to an adult.

We suggest that you select a relaxed atmosphere, and that you continue reading the stories only as long as the child remains interested in listening. You may wish to change the names, or the circumstances, or the objects identified in the stories to enhance their reality or to give the child a sense of personal involvement.

The children in these stories always do the right thing. Ideally, your child should respond to your question, "What would you do?"

For example, if the character's response to a situation is: "Jack said 'NO' and ran home and told his mom," you would want to elicit a similar response to your question, "What would you do?"

If your child says, "I'd do the same thing," simply repeat the character's response to the situation, "You'd say 'NO,' and you'd run home and tell me, right?"

This and other forms of playacting can be very valuable lessons for your child. Playacting serves as a kind of rehearsal in the event the child is ever confronted with a comparable real-life situation.

BILLY'S STORY

Billy walks home from school every day. It's not very far, and he likes to play in the leaves on the sidewalk. One day, a car stops near Billy. A lady in the car asks Billy if he wants a ride home. Billy knows that he should never get in a car without his mom's or dad's permission.

He says "NO," and he runs home and tells his mom about it.

What would you do?

MARY ANN'S STORY

Mary Ann went to the grocery store for her mother. They needed milk and bread and it was just a short walk to the store. Mary Ann liked going to the store because Mr. Philips, who ran the store, always made jokes with her.

When she left with the milk and bread, Mr. Wilson was standing in front of his barber shop next door. He called Mary Ann over and told her he wanted to give her a gift because she was so nice.

Mary Ann knew that she was not permitted
to take gifts or money from people unless it
was her birthday or her parents knew about
it.

She said, "NO thank you," and went home
and told her mom about what had happened.
What would you do?

BOBBY'S STORY

Bobby was playing touch football with his friends in the park one day. Bobby liked playing touch football. He was pretty good at catching passes, even when he had to dive for the football.

Bobby noticed that there was a man standing at the side of the field watching him and his friends playing. He asked his friends if anyone knew the man. No one did.

When the game was over, and everyone was going home, Bobby noticed that the man started talking to Michael, one of his friends. Michael was always the last to leave when the game was over, and he usually went home alone.

Bobby yelled to Michael: "Come on, Michael, you slowpoke, we're all going home together." And when Bobby got home, he told his mom and dad about the man hanging around their playing field.

What would you do?

ALICE'S STORY

Alice was in the playground one day with her friend Billy. They were playing a game on the climbing bars to see who could get to the top first.

Alice liked climbing on the bars. It was fun and she was good at it. But this time she tried to do it too fast. She slipped and fell. She didn't hurt herself when she landed on the ground, but she landed in a puddle, and got mud on her brand new jeans.

Billy had to go home, but Alice thought she should get some of the mud off her jeans first, and then go home. She went into the girls' restroom in the playground to clean her jeans.

A woman came in right behind her. The woman asked Alice if she could help clean her up. Alice said, "No, I can do it myself, thanks."

Then the woman asked if she could take Alice's picture. Alice thought, *This is pretty weird—someone wanting to take your picture in a restroom.*

Alice said "NO," and she ran out of the restroom, ran home, and told her mom what had happened.

What would you do?

DAVID'S STORY

David was playing his favorite game down
at the video arcade. He wasn't as good at
it as his friend Ray, but thanks to a little
practice, he was better than most of his friends.

David noticed that there was an older boy
watching him. David didn't know him.

After a while, the boy came over and said,
"Hey, you're pretty good at that. Let me buy
you a few games."

David didn't know why a stranger would want to pay for someone else's games, and he really wanted to be left alone.

David said, "No thanks, I'll buy my own games." The boy went away, and David continued to play. When he got home, he told his mom about the boy.

What would you do?

BETTY'S STORY

Betty was running down the street She was going to visit her friend Connie to watch their favorite television program together. She had asked her mom if it was O.K. Her mom and Connie's mom approved.

Betty was running so fast she didn't see a big crack in the sidewalk. Her foot hit it, and down she went, banging her knee on the curb. Suddenly, she felt a hand under her arm. It was a policeman helping her up.

"Are you okay?" he asked.

"My knee hurts," Betty said.

"Well, you just bruised it," the policeman said, "it's not bleeding. Why don't you sit down for a minute until it stops hurting?"

Betty sat on the curb. The pain quickly went away. Betty noticed that the policeman had his hand on her shoulder for a long time. It made her feel funny. "Thank you for helping me," she said, "but I don't want you to touch me anymore." Then she got up and went to Connie's house.

What would you do?

FREDDIE'S STORY

Freddie's dad was fixing a broken window one day when the phone rang. He said, "Will you answer that for me, Freddie? I'm too busy to do it myself."

Freddie answered the phone. It was a man asking for someone Freddie had never heard of. "I'm sorry," Freddie said, "you have the wrong number."

"Oh, I'm sorry," the man said, "what number did I get?"

Freddie knew that when people dial a wrong number, it's their fault, and they shouldn't ask what number they got.

When the man asked, "What number did I get?" Freddie said, "I'm sorry, you got a wrong number," and hung up the phone.

What would you do?

LAURA'S STORY

Laura's favorite subject in school was geography. She was crazy about it. She could recite the names of all the countries of South America and Europe. She liked maps, but she especially liked books with pictures of faraway places with interesting names.

Mr. Nelson was Laura's music teacher at school. He knew about Laura's interest in geography. One day in school, he said, "Laura, I have a wonderful picture book about South America at home. If you come to my house after school, I'll let you look at it."

Laura knew she wasn't allowed to go to
someone else's house without her mom's
permission. She told Mr. Nelson that.

He said, "Oh, that's O.K. We'll make it a
secret between us."

Laura knew that there is no reason for adults to have secrets with children. Laura said, "NO, I'm not allowed to go to anyone's house without my mom's permission."

When she got home, she told her mom what had happened with Mr. Nelson.

What would you do?

BRIAN'S STORY

One day Brian was walking along the street on his way home from school. He was deep in thought, trying to remember the words to a new song he liked.

Suddenly, a car pulled up to the curb just ahead of him. A man was driving. He beeped his horn, and said to Brian, "Son, can you tell me how to get to the Westbrook Overpass?"

Brian knew where the Westbrook Overpass was, but he also knew that if adults wanted directions, they should ask other adults.

Brian said, "NO, I can't help you," and kept on walking.
What would you do?

STEPHANIE'S STORY

One day in school, Stephanie felt sick. Her stomach hurt and she felt a little dizzy. Her teacher sent her to the school nurse's office.

The nurse, Mrs. Carmichael, was there alone. She asked Stephanie how she felt and was very sympathetic. She came out from behind her desk and sat very close to Stephanie.

Mrs. Carmichael said, "Here, just let me rub your stomach to make it feel better."

Stephanie knew that rubbing her stomach wasn't going to make it any better, and she knew that she had the right to say "NO" if anybody wanted to touch her in any way.

Stephanie said, "NO, I don't want you to touch me. I think I'd better just go home." What would you do?

RONNY'S STORY

Ronny was home alone one afternoon. His dad was at work and his mom had gone to the store to get some things for a birthday party the next day for one of Ronny's friends.

RING

The phone rang, and Ronny answered it. He thought it might be his friend Bert calling. Instead, it was a man who said he wanted to talk to Ronny's father.

Ronny said his father was at work. The man asked if Ronny was home alone.

Ronny's mom had told him he should
never tell anyone he was home alone. Ronny
told the man, "My mom can't come to the
phone right now. May I take a message?
She'll call you back."

What would you do?

BARBARA'S STORY

Barbara was going home one day from a Girl Scout meeting. At the meeting, everyone had made plans for their Girl Scout outing. Barbara loved the outings. She got together with her friends, and they slept in tents and cooked food on an open fire.

While Barbara was walking home, a man she knew from the neighborhood, Mr. Harris, came up to her and asked if he could take her picture.

Barbara knew that people don't come up to you and ask to take your picture for no reason. You take pictures when relatives and friends get together.

Barbara said "NO," and she ran home and told her parents about it.

What would you do?

TOMMY'S STORY

Tommy was in the playground one afternoon, shooting baskets by himself. His friends Eddie and Jay had gone home early, but Tommy still had a half hour before he had to go home for dinner. Tommy didn't mind playing by himself, because it gave him a chance to practice his shots.

A man was watching Tommy. The man said, "You've got a pretty good shot. Let me show you how you can make it better."

The man came through the gate onto the basketball court. Tommy knew that if he wanted coaching, he could ask his dad or his basketball coach at school.

70

Tommy picked up his basketball and said, "NO, I have to go home." He left the playground and hurried home.

What would you do?

TINA'S STORY

Tina was staying overnight at her friend Lucy's house. Her mom had said it was okay, and Lucy's mom had, too. Tina and Lucy had fun playing together with Lucy's dolls.

Lucy's mom and dad went out to a movie while the two girls were playing, and Lucy's big brother stayed at home to watch them.

Lucy's room was too small for the two girls to sleep together, so Tina slept in the guest bed downstairs. After Tina put her pajamas on and went to bed, Lucy's big brother came into the room and started saying strange things that made Tina feel uncomfortable.

Tina started to get a little scared, and at first she didn't know what to do. But Tina's mom and dad had told her that any time she felt scared or uncomfortable in someone else's house, she should call home. She knew she never had to ask anyone's permission to use the telephone when she was uncomfortable or scared.

Tina went to the telephone and called her mom and dad, and told them how she felt, and asked if they would come and take her home.

What would you do?

DOUGLAS'S STORY

One day in school, Douglas's teacher, Mr. Johnson, asked Douglas to stay after class for a few minutes.

When the other students left the room, Mr. Johnson told Douglas he might give him a bad grade in the class. Douglas said, "But I'm doing well in this class."

Mr. Johnson said, "It's up to me to decide if you are doing well or not." He walked over to Douglas's desk and put his arm around Douglas.

Douglas knew he had the right to say
"NO" if any adult touched him. He knew Mr.
Johnson did not have the right to take away
his good grade for no reason.

Douglas said, "I don't want you to touch me," and he got up from his desk and left the room. When Douglas got home, he told his parents what had happened.

What would you do?

KATE'S STORY

Kate was walking in the park one day. She watched a squirrel run across the grass and straight up the side of a tree. A man came up to her. He told her he was looking for his lost dog. He said he'd give her a dollar if she came with him to help him find the dog.

Kate is a smart girl. She knows that adults don't come to children for help. When they need help, they go to other adults.

Kate said "NO," and she ran away. When she got home she told her parents what had happened.

What would you do?

STEVEN'S STORY

One day Steven was playing his favorite
video game while his mother shopped next
door. There were some grown-ups playing too.
One of them left his friends and asked Steven if he wanted to go play a special video
game at his house.

Steven didn't even ask where he lived. Steven knew he should never go anywhere with a stranger.

Steven said "NO," and ran next door to find his mom to tell her what had happened.
What would you do?

CARMELLA'S STORY

Carmella loved her doll. She took it everywhere with her.

One evening, Carmella's parents went out and left her with a sitter, Rose Anne. The sitter said to Carmella, "You really love your doll, don't you?"

Carmella said, "Yes, she's my favorite."

Rose Anne said that if Carmella didn't do exactly as she was told, her doll would be taken away from her.

Carmella knew that her parents would never let anyone take away the things that belonged to her. She knew that even if someone took something of hers for a while, her parents would get it back.

Carmella said "NO" to Rose Anne, and when her parents came home, she told them what Rose Anne had said.

What would you do?

JIMMY'S STORY

Jimmy plays on a Little League baseball team. He plays shortstop, and once he hit a home run that won the game for his team.

One day, Jimmy's coach asked him to keep a secret about something. Jimmy knew that adults don't ask children to keep secrets. Secrets are for birthday presents and things like that. Secrets are for that special hiding place you and your friends have. Secrets are not for other things. You should be able to tell your mom and dad about anything that happens with adults.

Jimmy went home and told his dad what his coach had said.

What would you do?

JENNIFER'S STORY

Jennifer liked her Uncle Ted. He was nice, and he always kidded around with her. When he came to visit her house, he sometimes brought a little present for Jennifer.

One day, Uncle Ted came to the house when Jennifer's mom and dad weren't home. He said he was looking for Jennifer's dad. When Jennifer said her dad wasn't home, Uncle Ted said, "That's O.K.; I'll wait for him." He sat down in the living room and started talking to Jennifer.

Pretty soon, he started saying things that made Jennifer feel uncomfortable, and he touched her in a way that made her feel even worse.

Jennifer knew that if any adult did or said something that made her feel uncomfortable, she should say "NO."

Jennifer said "NO" to Uncle Ted, and
when her parents came home, she told them
what had happened.

What would you do?

JASON'S STORY

Jason was waiting outside school for his mom to come and take him home. It was raining hard, but Jason didn't mind. He had his rain slicker and his boots on, and he liked to watch the way the rain bounced in the puddles.

A car came along and stopped in front of Jason. There was a man in it, and he rolled down his window and said to Jason, "Hi, your mom sent me to bring you home."

Jason knew that his parents wouldn't send someone to get him from school without telling him.

Jason said "NO," and ran to tell an adult. When his mom came, he told her what had happened, too.

What would you do?

ANDREA'S STORY

Andrea was sitting on a park bench one day, waiting for her friend Carol to come along. It was a nice, sunny day, and Andrea was watching the cars and buses and trucks go by.

Suddenly, a man came up to Andrea and started a conversation. He was very pleasant, but Andrea wondered why an adult she didn't know would want to talk to her.

Then the man started asking her questions. Andrea's mom had told her not to talk to strangers. So Andrea said to the man, "I don't want to talk," and she got up from the bench and ran away. When she got home, she told her mom what had happened.

What would you do?

PHILIP'S STORY

Philip liked his next-door neighbor, Mr. Sanders. They both liked basketball a lot, and Mr. Sanders took Philip to a few games, where they had a good time. Mr. Sanders even introduced him to two pro basketball players, and that was a big thrill for Philip.

One evening, as they were leaving the arena, Mr. Sanders started making some strange suggestions to Philip about things that Philip would never think of doing.

What Mr. Sanders said made Philip very unhappy. He didn't want to lose Mr. Sanders's

friendship. But then Philip realized that maybe Mr. Sanders was being so nice to him only because he wanted Philip to do the things Mr. Sanders suggested.

Philip knew that real friends don't do things like that. He was sad about it, but he said "NO" to Mr. Sanders, and when he got home, he told his parents what had happened.

What would you do?

MARIA'S STORY

Maria and Janie were in day care together.
They were good friends. They liked all the
same things, such as finger painting. They
disliked all the same things, such as liver
for lunch.

One day, Maria noticed that Janie was acting
strangely. Marie asked Janie if she was okay.

Janie didn't answer. She just looked as though she was going to cry. "Janie, why don't you tell me what's the matter," Maria said.

Janie didn't say anything. She just pointed at Mr. Simpson, the caretaker.

Maria knew that if an adult is doing something that makes you or a friend very unhappy, you should tell your mom or dad—or someone else you can trust—about it.

Maria did just that. She went home and told her mom about Janie.

What would you do?

JACK'S STORY

Jack liked going into big department stores with his mom. He loved the toy section. He even liked the hardware and television and record sections. Jack was a department-store nut.

The trouble was, Jack would sometimes wander away from his mom when she took too long in some boring part of the store. Then he would get lost.

When Jack got lost, he knew he should go to a cash register and tell the people there that he had lost his mom.

One day, as usual, Jack got lost in a big
department store. A man came up to him
and said, "Are you lost, young man?" Jack
didn't say anything, but the man took him
by the arm and started to lead him away.

Jack knew what you should do when you get lost in a store. You should stay in one place and let the store people find your mom. Jack dropped to the floor and yelled as loud as he could, "This man isn't my dad."

That was the right thing to do, because the man hurried away.

What would you do?

MARCIA'S STORY

Marcia and her friend Cathy went to the movies to see a film they had been looking forward to. They went early so that they could sit in their favorite spot.

Just before the movie started, a man sat down right behind them. Marcia and Cathy could tell that he was watching them. Marcia said to Cathy, "Let's move." As the movie was starting, they went to the other side of the theater. In a few minutes, the man followed and sat behind them again.

Cathy whispered to Marcia, "I'm scared."
Marcia said, "Not me. I'm going to tell the
manager. We paid for this movie, and nobody
has the right to make us feel uncomfortable."

Marcia told the manager what had happened. He came down with his flashlight and forced the man to move. Marcia and Cathy didn't see the man again.

What would you do?

ALEX'S STORY

Alex had a job delivering newspapers. He rode through the neighborhood on his bike, tossing rolled-up newspapers onto his customers' steps.

Mr. Chambers was Alex's boss. He gave Alex his newspapers to deliver every day, and paid him once a week.

One day when Alex was alone with Mr. Chambers, waiting for his newspapers, Mr. Chambers started touching Alex. Alex told him to stop.

Mr. Chambers first told Alex that he might

take his delivery job away, and then he
threatened to hurt Alex.

Alex knew that if the newspaper people
knew what Mr. Chambers was doing, they
would fire him. He knew that if Mr. Chambers
hurt him, Mr. Chambers would be in really big
trouble.

Alex said, "NO, I don't want you to touch me." He took his newspapers and made his deliveries, and when he got home, he told his parents what had happened with Mr. Chambers.

What would you do?

BETSY'S STORY

Betsy was walking along the street one day, carrying her violin. She was on her way to Mrs. Johnson's house for her violin lessons. Betsy liked to play the violin, even though her little brother Johnny put his hands over his ears when she practiced.

A lady came up to her on the street. She said, "Oh, I played the violin too when I was your age. What's your name, young lady, and where do you live?" the woman asked.

Betsy knew that when strangers want to know your name and where you live, they

should ask your parents. Betsy just said, "I have to go now," and she hurried to Mrs. Johnson's house for her lessons.

Later, when she was home, she told her parents what had happened.
What would you do?

CHRISTOPHER'S STORY

Christopher's mother and father were going out to dinner and the movies. When Christopher's baby-sitter, Mrs. Connors, came, he was watching television. He said good night to his mom and dad when they left.

Later on, when Christopher was ready for bed, Mrs. Connors started telling him things about love and sex.

Christopher knew that no one was allowed
to tell him about such things except his mom
and dad. He told Mrs. Connors he didn't

want to hear about those things. The next day, when he woke up, he told his mom and dad what Mrs. Connors had talked about.

What would you do?

AMY'S STORY

Amy was at the swimming pool one day.
She enjoyed being there, although she didn't
like the way some of the bigger boys clowned
around at the pool. Some of them would
cannonball into the water, splashing water all
over the pool area.

Amy was learning how to swim. She was
practicing hard so she could show her dad
how much she had learned the next time he
came to the pool.

Pete, the lifeguard, saw Amy practicing.
"Hey, Amy," he said, "let me help you practice
your swimming."

Pete came over to Amy and held her up in the water while she practiced her swimming stroke. But soon he was touching Amy in a way that made her feel uncomfortable.

Amy knew that anytime anyone touched her in a way that she didn't like—no matter who that person was—she had the right to stop it by just saying "NO."

So she said, "NO, I don't want you to touch me," and she moved away and practiced swimming by herself.

What would you do?

JEFFREY'S STORY

Jeffrey was out riding his bike one day. It was a nice summer day and he was being very careful to stay away from places where there were cars.

He was just down the street from his home. Suddenly, he heard someone calling him, "Yoo hoo, Jeffrey!" It was a neighbor, Mrs. Smith. She was standing on her front lawn. "Hello, Mrs. Smith," Jeffrey said.

Mrs. Smith said, "I borrowed a dish from your mother last week. Would you be a dear and take it home for me? Come in the house while I find it."

Jeffrey knew that he was never allowed
to go inside someone else's house without his
parents' permission. "It's O.K., I'll wait
outside," he said. And he did.

What would you do?

JACQUELINE'S STORY

Jacqueline's mother isn't home when school lets out, so Jacqueline has her own key to get into her house.

One afternoon, Jacky was watching TV by herself. The phone rang and it was someone who wanted to know if Jacky was home alone. Jacky knows that she should never tell people she is alone.

Jacky said, "My mother is busy right now. Please call back later."

What would you say?